AF654323

Whispers of Eternity

A Symphony of Soulful Verses

"Embark on an eternal journey through the seasons of life and the depths of emotion, intricately woven with poetic reflections on the interconnectedness of all existence."

SHREE SHAMBAV

Whispers of Eternity:
A Symphony of Soulful Verses Series – II
Shree Shambav

Published by Shree Shambav, Tamil Nadu, India
Shree Shambav Ink & Imagination "Where Words Breathe and Imagination Soars"

First Edition, 2025

ISBN: 978-93-342-8554-3

Email:shreeshambav@gmail.com
Web:www.shambav.org

DEDICATION

"Isavasyam idam sarvam yat kim ca jagatyam jagat, tena tyaktena bhunjitha, ma gridhah kasyasvid dhanam"

To the Almighty,

the Divine Masters,

the family who listens,

and my parents who see –

your presence shapes the pages of my life's journey.

"Isavasyam idam sarvam yat kim ca jagatyam jagat"

Meaning: "God encompasses everything you perceive, see, or touch with your sense organs."

DISCLAIMER

"Whispers of Eternity: A Symphony of Soulful Verses Series - II" invites you to journey into the heart of human experience, exploring its intricate layers through a collection of poignant and thought-provoking poetry. This book seeks to offer a deep, soulful reflection on life, nature, and the vastness of existence, encouraging readers to engage with the verses in their own unique way, finding personal truths and insights that resonate with their own lived experiences.

With a foundation built on compassion, love, and care, the author endeavours to inspire readers to explore the deeper dimensions of their lives, gently guiding them toward a profound understanding of their own paths. Every word, every line, is an invitation to connect with the silent truths that echo through our lives—never to unsettle but to uplift and enlighten.

The journey through these verses is not about rigid interpretations or dogmas but about embracing the fluidity of life and the wisdom that arises from within. The content is a reflection of the author's personal perspective, offered as a source of inspiration, insight, and gentle guidance. Readers are invited to absorb, reflect, and adapt the message according to their own truths and experiences.

Above all, this book aims to inspire joy, connection, and meaningful living. It encourages you to cultivate a life of purpose, compassion, and integrity, embracing each moment with intentionality and grace. May the words within these pages light your way, as you embark on your personal journey of self-discovery, growth, and transformation. The path is yours to walk, and it is an honour to accompany you along the way.

This book is not a substitute for medical, psychological, or spiritual guidance. Readers are encouraged to seek support from qualified professionals where appropriate. The reflections and interpretations offered within these pages are subjective and symbolic, and they may touch upon emotionally sensitive topics such as loss, trauma, and inner transformation.

All characters, imagery, and emotional narratives are fictional or metaphorical unless otherwise stated. Any resemblance to actual persons, living or deceased, is purely coincidental.

Note - If any part of the book, in any sequence, hurts the reader's sentiments, it would be just out of a sheer accident not intentional

The River Within

Walk through life with a quiet heart, undisturbed by the clamor of the world. Let your presence speak in stillness, not in the need to be heard. Hold fast to your truths, but never raise them as swords—for the strongest soul is one who honors difference with grace. No title, no triumph can undo the pain of an unkind act; greatness is hollow when it leaves others broken.

Let your journey be guided not by applause but by the timeless whisper of the eternal. In a world of speed and gain, be the one who seeks the silence before creation—the pause before the breath, the stillness that births true knowing.

Live with a spirit open and vast, unburdened by ego, yet brimming with unseen light. Like a river, your strength is not in the ripples above, but in the depths that flow quietly beneath. That is where peace resides. That is where you truly are.

– Shree Shambav

EPIGRAM

"What the soul cannot speak in prose, it
sings in poetry—
and in that song, eternity whispers back."

– Shree Shambav

Whispers of Eternity

A Symphony of Soulful Verses

Shree Shambav

Shree Shambav is a 32x best-selling author renowned for his transformative works in personal development and spiritual growth.

Dear Cherished Readers

Dear Cherished Readers,

As I embark on this new literary voyage, my heart swells with profound gratitude and an overwhelming sense of connection. With deep emotion, I extend my heartfelt appreciation to each of you who has joined me on this journey.

With sincere warmth, I invite you to revisit the steps we have taken together through the pages of my earlier works. Our odyssey began with "Journey of Soul - Karma," a book that marked my first foray into the world of words and a testament to the raw passion that ignited my writing adventure.

The subsequent chapters of our shared journey unfolded through the enchanting tapestry of the *"Twenty + One"* series. With each page turned, it felt as though a brushstroke was added to the canvas of our collective imagination—stories and sentiments woven to echo within the quiet corners of your heart. These weren't just words; they were invitations to feel, to reflect, and to remember what truly matters.

And how can I not cherish the transformative path we walked together through the *"Life Changing Journey—Inspirational Quotes Series?"* Day by day, quote by quote, we ventured inward—into spaces often overlooked—to find wisdom in simplicity and light in life's shadows. Each reflection was offered as a gentle whisper of hope, a spark meant to uplift, inspire, and remind us that even in silence, the soul speaks.

The release of "Death - Light of Life and the Shadow of Death" promises to shed new light on the timeless mystery of death. Similarly, "Unleashing the Incredible Potential of Programming with Python - Optimum - PYTHON: Ultimate Guide for Beginners Series I" is poised to empower readers with newfound knowledge.

In addition, my technical book, OPTIMUM Python Series II - Exploring Data Structures and Algorithms, delves into advanced concepts in Python programming, offering a comprehensive guide for those seeking to deepen their understanding.

OPTIMUM – Python Power Series III is your essential guide to mastering the most powerful Python libraries for data science. From data manipulation and visualisation to machine learning, this book empowers you with practical tools to solve real-world challenges. Unleash your potential and transform the way you work with data.

Shree Shambav expands his artistic repertoire with "*Whispers of Eternity: 150 Plus - A Symphony of Soulful Verses,*" a heartfelt exploration of the human experience. Alongside this, his "*Whispers of the Soul: A Journey Through Haiku*" distils profound insights into poignant verses. Together, these works showcase his versatility and mastery of soulful expression, inviting readers on a journey of self-discovery. Through his poetry, he weaves a rich tapestry of emotion that resonates deeply with the heart.

Shree Shambav's latest works—*Learn to Love Yourself: A Journey of Discovering Inner Beauty and Strength Through 10 Transformative Rules, The Power of Letting Go: Embrace Freedom and Happiness, A Journey of Lasting Peace—are true treasures of self-discovery, The Entitlement Trap: Get Over It, Get On, Whispers of a Dying Soul: Unspoken Regrets and Unlived Dreams, Whispers of Silence - Unlocking Inner Power through Stillness, The Power of Words: Transforming Speech, Transforming Lives, The Art of Intentional Living: Minimalism for a Life of Purpose, Awakening the Infinite:The Power of Consciousness in Transforming Life, Beyond the Veil: A Journey Through Life After Death series, Bonds Beyond Blood - Where love builds bridges, and bonds defy blood., and A Journey into Spiritual Maturity - 12 Golden Rules for Inner Transformation.*

In addition to these works, Shree Shambav has recently ventured into astrology with the release of Astrology Unveiled – Foundations of Ancient

Wisdom Series I to VI, expanding into the realm of metaphysics. These books explore the foundational principles of Vedic astrology, offering readers a rich and practical understanding of this ancient wisdom.

Your unwavering support, enthusiasm to immerse yourself in my writings, and readiness to embark on these journeys with me have been my greatest sources of inspiration. Your input has been a beacon guiding me through the creation process, moulding these stories into containers of passion, emotion, knowledge, and resonance.

As I unveil this new narrative before you, know that your presence, insights, and shared moments have been my companions. The path we have walked together is etched in the annals of my creative evolution, and it's an honour beyond words to have you by my side once more.

Here's to the readers who have illuminated my path with their presence, who have embraced my stories with open hearts, and who have woven themselves into the very fabric of my literary world. Our journey has been a symbiotic dance of writer and reader, a harmony of souls brought together by the magic of storytelling.

With a heart brimming with appreciation and eyes glistening with anticipation, I extend my deepest gratitude for your unwavering support. Thank you for the memories, the shared emotions, and the countless hours spent in the worlds we've crafted together. As we step into this new adventure, let's continue to explore, feel, and discover the boundless horizons that words can unveil.

Warmly,

Shree Shambav

Suggested Reads

FROM BEST-SELLING AUTHOR

Endorsements

"Whispers of Eternity: A Symphony of Soulful Verses – Series II" is not merely a collection of poems—it is an intimate unfolding of the human spirit. With lyrical grace and profound emotional insight, this book tenderly guides readers through the landscapes of love, solitude, grief, desire, transformation, and divinity.

Each chapter becomes a sacred threshold: *Whispers in Moonlight* stirs forgotten emotions, *Ripples of Solitude* echoes the beauty of stillness, and *Celestial Conversations* draws us into communion with the infinite. The verses are as timeless as they are timely—an offering to anyone navigating the complexities of the heart, the ache of longing, or the awe of awakening.

This is poetry that listens. Poetry that holds. Poetry that mirrors the soul back to itself.

In a world often rushing past the subtle, *Whispers of Eternity* invites us to pause, to feel deeply, and to remember what it means to be profoundly, vulnerably human.

It is a symphony not just of words but of wisdom—softly powerful, eternally resonant.

— Lalitha Advocate

About the Author

Shree Shambav is an internationally acclaimed, best-selling author, inspirational speaker, artist, philanthropist, life coach, and entrepreneur. A world record holder, his deep passion for music led him to create soul-stirring albums, drawing inspiration from his celebrated poetry collection, Whispers of Eternity. His profound insights have sparked deep personal transformations, guiding countless individuals toward self-discovery, purposeful living, and authenticity.

With an extraordinary ability to unlock human potential, Shree empowers individuals to break through limitations and embrace their highest selves. His writings, lectures, and compassionate guidance continue to uplift lives, fostering resilience, mindfulness, and personal growth.

Shree Shambav is a 32x best-selling author celebrated for his profound contributions to personal development and spiritual growth.

Shree Shambav's literary journey took flight with the celebrated Journey of Soul - Karma, where he delved into the depths of human experience to unveil profound insights. Garnering recognition through multiple literature awards, his repertoire includes esteemed works, such as the Twenty + One Series and the enlightening Life Changing Journey – Inspirational Quotes series.

As a distinguished alumnus of the Indian Institute of Management and the National Institute of Technology, Shree Shambav brings a wealth of corporate acumen from his tenure in multinational corporations. His most recent publications, including Unveiling the Enigma, Death - Light of Life and the Shadow of Death and Optimum – Power Python Series I, Series II and Series III, demonstrate his mastery of both the literary and technical spheres.

Shree Shambav expands his artistic repertoire with "*Whispers of Eternity: 150 Plus - A Symphony of Soulful Verses*," a heartfelt exploration of the human experience. Alongside this, his "*Whispers of the Soul: A Journey Through Haiku*" distils profound insights into poignant verses. Together, these works showcase his versatility and mastery of soulful expression, inviting readers on a journey of self-discovery. Through his poetry, he weaves a rich tapestry of emotion that resonates deeply with the heart.

Shree Shambav's latest works—*Learn to Love Yourself: A Journey of Discovering Inner Beauty and Strength Through 10 Transformative Rules, The Power of Letting Go: Embrace Freedom and Happiness, A Journey of Lasting Peace—are true treasures of self-discovery, The Entitlement Trap: Get Over It, Get On, Whispers of a Dying Soul: Unspoken Regrets and Unlived Dreams, Whispers of Silence - Unlocking Inner Power through Stillness, The Power of Words: Transforming Speech, Transforming Lives, The Art of Intentional Living: Minimalism for a Life of Purpose, Awakening the Infinite:The Power of Consciousness in Transforming Life, Beyond the Veil: A Journey Through Life After Death series, Bonds Beyond Blood - Where love builds bridges, and bonds defy blood., and A Journey into Spiritual Maturity - 12 Golden Rules for Inner Transformation.*

In addition to these works, Shree Shambav has recently ventured into astrology with the release of Astrology Unveiled – Foundations of Ancient

Wisdom Series I to VI, expanding into the realm of metaphysics. These books explore the foundational principles of Vedic astrology, offering readers a rich and practical understanding of this ancient wisdom.

Shree Shambav established the Ayur Rakshita Foundation, which is dedicated to promoting boundless growth, universal fraternity, and environmental protection. The charity helps diverse communities while working for societal progress.

To learn more about Shree Shambav and his works, visit his website at www.shambav.org. For information about the Ayur Rakshita Foundation and its initiatives, visit www.shambav-ayurrakshita.org.

Let's Follow him on Social Media: **@shreeshambav**

PREFACE

Whispers of Eternity: A Symphony of Soulful Verses – Series II

There are moments in life that cannot be contained by prose—moments where the soul speaks in silence, where feeling becomes form, and where the unseen finds expression in verse. *Whispers of Eternity* was born from such moments. It is not merely a collection of poems, but a journey—a symphony of the soul's quiet revolutions and eternal questions.

Each poem in this second series stands as a testament to transformation, a mirror to emotion in its rawest essence. As the seasons of the human spirit shift—through love and loss, stillness and storm—this book traces their echoes with reverence and insight.

Whispers in Moonlight: A Prelude to Emotion opens the door to the quiet longing that dwells beneath our waking lives. In **Ripples of Solitude**, silence is not empty—it is a canvas upon which the soul paints its truest hues. **Ephemeral Eternity** seeks permanence in fleeting seconds, reminding us that eternity often hides in a heartbeat.

Resonance of Love delves into the sacred pulse that binds us, while **Shadows of Grief** gives voice to sorrow with gentle, tender metaphor. In **Whirlwind of Passion**, desire is a fire that both warms and consumes, fierce yet tender. **Resilient Reverie** tells of beauty born from hardship, of blossoms that rise through cracks in stone.

In **Celestial Conversations**, the divine is no longer distant—it is the breath between words, the space between stars, the silence after prayer. And **Serenade of Seasons** closes the journey with nature's rhythm, a final reminder that life itself is a poem—unfolding, returning, evolving.

This book is a sacred invitation—not just to read but to remember. To feel without fear. To surrender to stillness. To hear your eternal whisper through the quiet notes of these verses.

As you turn these pages, may you recognise your voice in their rhythms. May they accompany you through the vastness of inner worlds. And may they remind you that your presence, your pain, your passion—are all part of an everlasting song.

Welcome to the second symphony.

— *With soul and silence,*

Shree Shambav

INTRODUCTION

To the Seeker of Silent Truths and Echoes of the Eternal

Poetry, at its essence, is not crafted merely with words—it is sculpted from the breath between them, from the ache beneath silence, from the shimmer of a moment caught between memory and becoming. *Whispers of Eternity: A Symphony of Soulful Verses – Series II* is not simply a collection of poems; it is a journey into the hidden corridors of the human soul. It is an invitation to witness the sacred unfolding of the self across time, emotion, loss, love, and the divine.

Each chapter in this book is a thread in a greater tapestry—a symphony composed not with instruments but with the resonance of the heart.

Whispers in Moonlight: A Prelude to Emotion begins the journey, capturing the delicate tremors of feeling that stir beneath moonlit skies. Here, vulnerability is not weakness—it is the doorway to presence.

Ripples of Solitude: Echoes in Silence guides you through the still chambers of aloneness, where silence does not echo emptiness but rather the intimate music of self-contemplation.

Ephemeral Eternity: Moments Frozen in Verse hold time in suspension, revealing that the fleeting is not lesser than the eternal—in fact, it is the very soul of it. The smallest moments often leave the deepest impressions.

Resonance of Love: Melodies of the Soul celebrates love not as possession or perfection but as the echo that remains long after the touch has passed. Love, in this space, is not a story—it is a song still being written by the heart.

Shadows of Grief: Mourning in Metaphor is a brave descent into the places where loss resides. These poems do not seek to resolve sorrow but to honour it—to hold grief like a sacred companion who speaks in metaphor when language fails.

Whirlwind of Passion: Embers of Desire ignites the fire within—the force that fuels creativity, longing, rebellion, and transformation. Desire here is not confined to romance but extends to life itself.

Resilient Reverie: Blooms Amidst Adversity is the chapter of strength. Not the loud, armoured kind—

but the quiet blooming through cracks, the dream that endures even when the world forgets it.

Celestial Conversations: Dialogues with the Divine lifts the veil between the earthly and the eternal. These verses are prayers, questions, moments of surrender—where the human meets the infinite in silence and awe.

Finally, **Serenade of Seasons: Poetry in Nature's Rhythm** returns us to the original poet—nature. Through her cycles and sighs, we are reminded of the rhythm we too are made of. To listen to the seasons is to remember ourselves.

This book was written not to explain life, but to feel it deeply. It is for the ones who have stood in the storm and waited for a whisper. For the ones who have forgotten and the ones who are learning to remember. For the ones who know that even in silence, the soul sings.

As you turn these pages, may you find echoes of your own journey. May these verses hold you the way moonlight holds the sea—with gentleness, with rhythm, and with reverence.

With a heart wide open,

Shree Shambav

PROLOGUE

When Silence Became Song

There are moments in life when language becomes too small to hold what we feel—when sorrow stretches wider than words, and joy rises higher than the sky of thought. It is in those spaces, where reason falters and emotion overflows, that poetry is born.

This book was not merely written—it was *remembered.* Remembered from the depths where longing dwells and from the heights where grace brushes against human skin. Each poem is a whisper from that space between—the threshold where the eternal meets the ephemeral.

Whispers of Eternity: A Symphony of Soulful Verses – Series II continues a sacred exploration that began not on the page but in the heartbeat of lived moments. It is a collection sculpted from moonlight and shadow, from loss and longing, from the ache to understand what it means to *be*—to be tender, to be resilient, to be divine, and still, deeply human.

This is a book about what lingers after silence. About the stories we carry not in memory but in marrow. About the soul's quiet voice that rises when the world grows still.

Each chapter unfolds like a movement in a symphony—a deepening of the melody that is life:

Whispers in Moonlight: A Prelude to Emotion captures the breath before the first tear, the hush before the heart speaks.

Ripples of Solitude: Echoes in Silence walks with the quiet weight of loneliness, revealing how stillness can hold the loudest truths.

Ephemeral Eternity: Moments Frozen in Verse invites us to see the eternal within the fleeting, the timeless in the transient.

Resonance of Love: Melodies of the Soul weaves tender threads between hearts—love in its many forms, aching and alive.

Shadows of Grief: Mourning in Metaphor does not shy away from sorrow but holds it gently, like a friend who knows your name.

Whirlwind of Passion: Embers of Desire burns with longing—not just of the body, but of the spirit aching to become.

Resilient Reverie: Blooms Amidst Adversity honours the quiet miracle of endurance, of blooming where no one thought beauty could grow.

Celestial Conversations: Dialogues with the Divine lifts the veil, letting the reader hear the hush of prayer, the echo of stars in the soul.

Serenade of Seasons: Poetry in Nature's Rhythm grounds the journey in the sacred pulse of the earth—where every season teaches us how to live, how to die, and how to begin again.

This is not a book to be rushed. It is to be *felt*. Let it rest in your hands. Let it rise in your breath. Let it echo in the silent places you've tried to forget.

And when you read—may you find pieces of your own story gently reflected in these pages, not as answers, but as companions.

For somewhere within us all, the eternal whispers. This is merely a listening.

CONTENTS

Whispers in Moonlight

A Prelude to Emotion

"In Nature's cycle, we find profound poetry of existence, where birth, death, and rebirth compose the verses of life's timeless song."

- *Shree Shambav*

Eternal Memories

Time passes like the wind, whispering stories untold,
Memories linger as if they were only yesterday's gold.
Filled with joy and sorrow, they flood our senses whole,
Each moment is etched deeply within our soul.

Our dearest angel, born with a celestial light,
We thanked the divine for this gift so bright.
Prayers of gratitude, for happiness she brought,
Yet her journey ended swiftly, leaving our hearts distraught.

Your curious questions, a constant in our days,
Now echo silently in the empty halls and quiet ways.
Your laughter, your play, your tender cry,
Once filled this house, now it's silent and dry.

But your love, your precious memories, they stay,
Guiding us through each challenging day.
Though your absence leaves a void so deep,
In our souls, your spirit forever we'll keep.

If tears could build a stairway, and memories pave a lane,
We'd walk to where you are, to bridge this sorrow and pain.

For you, our lost angel, forever in our hearts you reside,

In the eternal, embrace where love and memories abide.

A River of Tears

Beneath the moon's soft silver glow,
Lies a heart the world may never know.
Its joys, its pains, its hidden fears,
Pour silently into a river of tears.

Each droplet falls, a story untold,
Of dreams once bright, now dimmed and cold.
Yet in their shimmer, truths ignite,
A fragile beauty bathed in night.

For tears are not a sign of weak,
But courage is found when words can't speak.
A silent hymn, a soul laid bare,
A testament to love and care.

They trace the paths of broken hearts,
Of endings met and fresh new starts.
From depths of sorrow, hope takes flight,
Through streams of tears that cleanse the night.

So let them fall, those sacred streams,
For every tear births kinder dreams.
And in their flow, the heart will find,
A gentle peace to soothe the mind.

In the quiet, where tears reside,
The soul's true essence dares to abide.
A tender gift, these drops of grace,
Reflections of our truest place.

The Moon Within

The moon is a dream that guides the tides,
With gentle glow, it silently abides.
There is a moon within me, too,
A quiet glow that gently moves,

Flowing with the rhythm of my thoughts and dreams,
Waking the silence, where the light still gleams.
It waxes, wanes, a silver glow,
Casting light on shadows below.

In its calm embrace, I find relief,
A sanctuary for my soul's belief.
A beacon of peace, guiding through the night,
Leading me onward, back to light.

Hope rises in cracks where despair once lay,
Silent seeds sprouting, night turns to day.
Each phase a reminder, a gentle refrain,
That even in darkness, light can reign.

The moon whispers, soft and near,
Calling me to rise, to cast off fear.
In the cycles of my heart, I find my place,
Strength in stillness, peace in grace.

With every phase, I am reborn,
A quiet journey, no longer torn.
The moon within, a steady guide,
A light that leads me, deep inside.

Dissolve

To rise anew, one must let go,
Like caterpillars wrapped in sleep.
They melt within the dark below,
To earn the wings they're meant to keep.

The gold is cast in fire's breath,
Its shape is undone, its form erased.
Yet through that blaze of living death,
It shines anew, refined by grace.

So too must we release the mold—
The parts that clung, the self we knew—
To step into a life more bold,
Where all we are comes into view.

It hurts to lose what once was "me,"
Yet greater still is what unfolds,
A soul unshaped by certainty,
But carved by trust the silence holds.

To bloom, we must be brave and bare—
To break, dissolve, and not resist.
Only through loss are we made rare,
And find the light we once dismissed.

The Grace of Becoming

To cling too tightly to what's been
Is to resist the tide within.
The soul was made to shift and grow—
Not dwell in where it once had been.

The seed must crack to greet the sun,
Its shell undone by unseen light.
So must we break to rise anew—
Each fracture born of sacred fight.

The pain of change may pierce us deep,
But silence bears a deeper cost.
To stagnate is to slowly fade,
To breathe and yet remain half-lost.

The whisper stirs, both soft and near:
"Become, evolve—go past the known."
And when we trust that quiet voice,
We walk a path that feels like home.

For grace will never bid us stay
Nor bind us to the shrinking shore.
It calls us where we dared not look—
To be what we were made for more.

Ripples of Solitude

Echoes in Silence

"As solitude envelops us in its gentle embrace, the echoes of silence resonate with the depths of our being, revealing truths that only solitude can unveil."

- *Shree Shambav*

The Unspoken Heart

I don't know why she's leaving,
Or where she's going to go.
But for sure she has a reason,
And I am left in the shadows of my woe.

For twenty years, she lived opposite my door,
We grew up together, sharing life's lore.
Through sunny days and rainy nights,
We played and laughed, our hearts alight.

We went to school, side by side,
In joy and sorrow, our spirits are tied.
Now she's gone, and I'm left here,
With a heart full of unspoken fears.

For twenty years, I watched and waited,
Hoping for a moment, a chance was created.
To tell her how I truly feel,
To share a love, deep and real.

Now she's gone, waiting for twenty years,
To tell her how I feel, maybe to calm my fears.
To get a second glance, to bridge the silent gap,
But now she's gone, and there's no turning back.

Her laughter echoes in my mind,
Her smile, a distant, cherished light.
In every moment, her absence is felt,
In every heartbeat, her presence lingers.

I wonder where her path has led,
If she remembers the times we shared.
Does she know my heart's silent cry,
The love I never dared to voice?

Now, as the days grow long and nights grow cold,
I sit by my window, and memories unfold.
Hoping one day she'll return,
And I'll finally find the courage to speak.

For in this life, we often wait,
For moments lost, for twists of fate.
And though she's gone, I hold on tight,
To the hope that one day, I'll make it right.

Still waiting to express the love I never spoke,
The unspoken words, the silent hope that broke.
In the shadows of time, my heart remains true,
Yearning to share what she never knew.

Life moves on, but my heart stays in that place,
Hoping for a moment, a chance to embrace.
Though she's gone, my feelings remain,
An eternal longing, a sweet, unspoken pain.

The Silence We Are

Essence is emptiness, wide and clear,
A breathless space where none appear.
Thoughts melt like mist before the day,
As dawn light washes doubt away.
It waits beneath the noise and name—
The silent pulse from which we came.

The surface stirs, the shadows play,
Illusions dancing through the day.
Yet all we chase is made to fade,
Like footprints lost where waves have laid.
But stillness births a boundless peace,
Where love flows on, and clinging ceases.

No anchor there, no cage, no chain,
Just hearts unburdened by the strain.
For grasping turns to dust and flame,
When we forget, we're not the name.
Desire burns, then leaves us bare—
It seeks but never finds us there.

In fleeting things we often trust,
Yet joy decays, and gold turns rust.
The world deceives with painted truth—
It steals the wonder born in youth.
Yet emptiness, so vast and wide,
Becomes the home where truths abide.

It's not a void, nor hollow tomb,
But fertile dark—a sacred womb.
The source beneath the storm and skin,
The home we left, yet hold within.
From silence shaped, we rise and roam,
Yet always hear that call toward home.

So let the noise and hunger cease,
And rest within the breath of peace.
No need to prove, no mask to wear—
Just be the stillness always there.
Return to what you've always been—
The vast, the quiet, deep within.

The Dreamer's Awakening

Eyes closed, and in the hush of sacred stillness,
it was felt—not as a thought, fleeting and weightless,
but as truth, woven into the marrow of being.

"What reality will be created?"

No longer a wanderer adrift in the vast unknown,
not apart from the universe—
but the rhythm of its breath,
the quiet pulse between silence and song.

The ocean—
depths unfathomed, tides unbroken,
cradling both storm and stillness
in the arms of eternity.

The wave—
rising, falling, surrendering to motion,
never lost, only becoming,
always returning home.

The dream—

woven from whispers of stardust and longing,

a vision shaped by light unseen,

soft as dawn, infinite as dusk.

And the dreamer—

eyes closed, yet seeing everything,

not waiting for destiny,

but daring to create it.

Where Words Fail, Music Speaks

When the mind is lost in haze,
Control dissolves in restless days.
When the mind is weak and torn,
Every trial feels forlorn.
Where words fail, does music speak?

When the mind stands firm and tall,
Challenges seem soft and small.
When the mind is fierce and strong,
Every storm will turn to song.
Where words fail, does music speak?

Life will teach through joy and pain,
Letting go is loss and gain.
Guilt, regret, or love held tight,
Fade like echoes in the night.
Where words fail, does music speak?

Change will come, a tide untamed,
Fought to keep, yet fought to wane.
Still, its rhythm shapes the way,
Only change will ever stay.
Where words fail, does music speak?

Don't resist the winds of change,
Now's the time to turn the page.
Free yourself from weight once known,
Let the future guide you home.

Where words fail, does music speak?

The Truth Beneath the Noise

You are not what your mind insists,
Not all its echoes, loud and near.
You are not shaped by fleeting thoughts,
Nor bound within the voice of fear.

You are not every fall you've faced,
Nor every doubt that drew you low.
These shadows come, then fade like mist—
They do not steal your truest glow.

The fears that knock with heavy hands,
The whispered lies, the false disguise—
They cannot reach the deeper self
That watches still behind your eyes.

For underneath the noise and strain,
Beyond the storms the mind can weave,
There lies a silence, calm and clear—
A truth the heart can still believe.

So pause, and breathe, and turn within,
Let every mask and shadow fall.
You are the light beneath the dark—
The one who sees, beneath it all.

The Bridge of Trust

When doubt begins to cloud your mind,
You pause and question every way.
Each step you fear to take or try
Let's quiet dreams begin to fray.

When hesitation holds you still,
You drift from what you're meant to be.
The voice that called with open hands
Now fades across a distant sea.

But trust is not a boastful cry,
Nor pride that wears a hollow crown.
It is the calm within the storm,
A hand that lifts, not lets you down.

It is the knowing deep inside,
Unmoved by all the world's disguise—
That you are held, and you are whole,
Beyond all doubt, beneath all lies.

The road is long, the skies may break,
And winds may howl without a name—
But if you trust your inner flame,
You'll walk through fire and rise through flame.

The bridge may shake, the night may fall,
And shadows blur the path ahead—
Yet if you walk with trust as guide,
Your soul will rise where angels tread.

Where Love Still Sings

The loving heart in whispers low,
Sings lullabies through threads of light.
It holds you close where sorrows flow,
And melts the chill of endless night.

A haven wrapped in quiet grace,
It found me through the hush of pain.
The child I was, no name, no face—
Still stood through storms and wept in rain.

No soul had told me love could heal,
That arms could soothe what fear had burned,
That wounds we hide, yet always feel,
Could bloom where gentler truths are learned.

You may have begged, you may have cried,
Yet love will meet you where you lie.
Where could the light from you divide?
It bends to you—it cannot die.

When clouds of shade in silence blend,
I see no fault, no wrong, no shame.
Each hue, each scar, is not the end—
But part of love's undying flame.

So hush, dear, sleep—the night is kind,
The voice once feared now softly sings.
The past is not what you must find—
But love that rises, folds its wings.

Ephemeral Eternity

Moments Frozen in Verse

"In the fleeting dance of time, we find eternity captured within the delicate folds of moments, each verse a testament to the timeless beauty of existence."

- *Shree Shambav*

Divine Symphony

You are my life, you are my body,
You are my earthly relation, oh Mother.
You bore me within, shared your blood,
Gave me your breath, and shaped my soul.

Mother, you are the symphony of kindness,
A river of compassion flowing endlessly.
A single tear from your eyes
Can make the seas roar with shared sorrow.

I have not seen the Divine,
You are the only divinity I know.
Your affection and your sacred feet
Are the very heaven I seek on earth.

I often wonder why the Divine created mothers,
And I found the answer to the world's design:
He created the sky, the earth, the air, the light,
But the world found no peace until He made you.

In your arms, I find solace and love,
In your eyes, the reflection of the universe.
Your whispers are the songs of angels,
Your touch, the gentle embrace of the divine.

Mother, you are the dawn that breaks my night,
The beacon that guides me through life's storm.
Your love is an eternal flame,
Illuminating the darkest paths with warmth and light.

You are the essence of all that is pure,
The embodiment of grace and sacrifice.
In your presence, I am whole,
In your love, I find my place in the world.

Mother, you are the masterpiece of creation,
The answer to the Divine's quest for compassion.
In you, I see the perfection of His love,
I find the truest form of peace.

Forever, I am in awe of your strength,
Grateful for the life you gave me.
For in your embrace, I find my home,
In your heart, I find my eternal sanctuary.

Am I the Wind or the Feather?

Am I the wind that sweeps the skies,
Untamed, unseen, where freedom lies?
A force that roams with restless flight,
A whispered breath in endless night.

Or am I but the fragile feather,
Falling softly, bound to tether,
Carried by the whims of fate,
Guided by the winds that wait?

I feel the gusts, I hear the call,
Yet often wonder, do I stand tall?
Am I the one who shapes the air,
Or just a passenger, unaware?

The wind, roars with endless might,
A conqueror of day and night,
Yet the feather dances with such grace,
Leaving beauty in its gentle trace.

WHISPERS OF ETERNITY

In me, I see both sides collide—
The strength to soar, the will to glide.
Am I the wind that moves the earth,
Or the feather that gives it worth?

I search the sky, the ground, the sea,
To find what lies inside of me.
Am I the storm that rages free,
Or the quiet stillness that longs to be?

Perhaps in truth, I am both parts,
The winds that push and the feathered heart.
For we are all a blend of fate,
Of power, softness, love, and weight.

So here I stand, between the two,
The wind that howls and the feather's hue.
For both must dance, both must entwine,
In the depths of me, they both align.

I Have Learned

I have lived—truly lived—
In nature's embrace, so vast, so wide,
Where rivers hum and mountains bide,
The whispering winds, the golden light,
A world that shimmers, pure and bright.

I have danced in the silver rain,
Laughed with birds in joyful strain,
Chased butterflies in fields so wide,
Watched dragonflies in gentle glide,
Found solace where the old trees hide.

I have loved—so deep, so true,
My parents' warmth, their love that grew,
The guiding hands of teachers wise,
The laughter bright in childhood skies,
The fleeting joy that never dies.

But I have lost—oh, how I've wept,
Felt love dissolve where memories slept,
Watched dear ones fade like twilight's hue,

Regrets that linger, deep and true,
For words unsaid and paths askew.

I have stumbled in my way,
Let my heart in shadows stray,
Hurt with words I left unmeant,
Trusted hands that came and went,
Lost in dreams that came and went.

Yet, in ruin, wisdom grew,
Pain revealed a brighter view,
Each sorrow carved a deeper space,
Each lesson held a warm embrace,
Each fall became a step to grace.

And now I walk with open eyes,
Not bound by fear, nor tangled ties,
Not scared to love, not scared to lose,
Not trapped by paths I did not choose,
For I have learned—I will not bruise.

Wings of Light

Let me open my wings and rise with the dawn,
Like a bird that knows no chains, no fear, no end.
I long to soar where the sky kisses the earth,
To dance in the breath of the boundless wind.

Oh, let not darkness steal my spark,
Nor sorrow shroud my beating heart.
I was not made to echo the past,
But to sing my truth, to make it last.

The rivers whisper, the moonlight sighs,
The stars weave dreams in endless skies.
Oh, let me dance with sunlit beams,
And hold the heavens in my dreams.

I long to chase the silver rain,
To waltz with winds that call my name.
Oh, let me touch the fleeting bow,
And bathe in midnight's gentle glow.

WHISPERS OF ETERNITY

Let the clouds wrap me in their mist,
Let lightning etch my soul's own twist.
Like rivers carving paths untold,
Unbound, unbroken—I unfold.

May the winds carry my unspoken dreams,
May colours flood the canvas of my soul.
I am not bound by earth nor time,
For I was born to rise, to shine, to fly.

Resonance of Love

Melodies of the Soul

"Like the gentle caress of a familiar melody, love permeates the soul, leaving behind a trail of resonant chords that linger in the heart long after the song has ended, a timeless echo of the soul's connection."

- *Shree Shambav*

Embracing Self-Love

In the garden of your soul, a tender seed,
Nurture it with love, for that's all you need.
Embrace the art of caring, let joy unfurl,
For within your soul's embrace lies the world.

Self-love, a spark, ignites the way,
A gentle ember, lighting night to day.
Boundless happiness, a path anew,
In the warmth of self-love, find your true view.

Within your embrace, discover grace,
For you are the cosmos in this space.
A microcosm of the grand design,
Reflecting stars in your soul's divine.

What you seek within, you'll find without,
In the depths of self, remove all doubt.
Search within; the answers abide,
For truth and wisdom in you reside.

Let your love be a beacon, shining bright,
Guiding others through the darkest night.
In nature's symphony, find your part,
For in self-acceptance, heal your heart.

In nature's symphony, each creature sings,
Embracing its essence, the joy it brings.
Yet in the human heart, a struggle begins,
To love oneself, where true freedom begins.

So let us learn from nature's song,
To love ourselves, where we belong.
For in the art of nurturing our soul,
Lies the essence of joy, making us whole.

A Song of Waiting and Hope

In the vast expanse of time, I patiently await,
Just a fleeting moment, your presence to sate.
Your memories flow like rivers, deep and wide,
Each gust of wind, your essence by my side.

In the symphony of nature, your laughter rings clear,
With every chirping bird, your smile draws near.
My mind, a canvas, painted with your grace,
In every passing moment, your presence I embrace.

When will our paths converge, my heart cries out,
Does your soul yearn, in silence, without doubt?
In your absence, my love grows ever strong,
A beacon in the darkness, where you belong.

But alas, I am but mortal, with no wings to soar,
No eyes to glimpse the beauty I adore.
Yet love transcends, beyond earthly strife,
Boundless and eternal, across the span of life.

Your arrival, a radiant light in my existence,
Yet, like a fleeting shadow, you vanish in an instance.
But I'll wait, with unwavering devotion true,
Until the day I'm blessed, once more, by you.

Echoes of Reverence

In the silence of inquiry, young Avinash queried,
"Why care for aged kin, frail and weary?"
The monk, with eyes that bore the weight of ages,
Answered with love's wisdom, through life's stages.

"When you speak of mothers, Avinash dear,
Speak with reverence, for their treasures are rare.
We label them burdens, deem them frail and weak,
Forgetting their nurturing, gentle and meek."

"Lost are their hopes in our ungrateful sighs,
Lost hopes in children, whom they raised to the skies.
We owe them more than fleeting glances, see,
To uplift and restore, to let their spirits be free."

"Even if they seem as adversaries in strife,
In their hearts, always, they wish for our life.
They measure their worth in our victories grand,
In each triumph, they extend a loving hand."

"They are beacons of love, unwavering and true,
In every circumstance, their blessings ensue.
A child's role is known, pivotal and bright,
Yet the presence of parents, equally right."

"They're not just old, but wisdom's wealth untold,
Not weary, but tireless in love's stronghold.
Not mere, but pure in intentions bold,
Not burdened, but bearers of life's manifold."

"Let them not be the last in life's tender embrace,
But the bedrock of kinship, firm in place.
A home without elders, barren and bare,
Like a tree without branches, in need of repair."

"For they are life's colours, in its grand design,
The brilliance of butterflies dances divine.
A home without elders, whispers a plea,
From cradle's warmth to final destiny."

"So cherish them dearly, from birth to the grave,
For they gave us life, our souls they save.
In their presence, find breath and dreams anew,
They are life's fountain, forever true."

Thus spoke the monk, in wisdom profound,
Guiding Avinash where grace is found.
In the monastery's sacred embrace,
He learned to honour his parents' lasting grace.

Unwavering Love

She loves me even when I don't love back,
Her heart's embrace fills every lack.
She stands by me when others take my time,
Her love is constant, pure, and truly sublime.

Her concern is my happiness, night and day,
She calls me each evening, come what may.
Even when unwell, she hides her pain,
Not wanting to burden me with her strain.

She dreams of my future, not lavish spending,
Her love, a beacon, is never-ending.
She loves me when I'm undeserving,
Her pride in me, forever serving.

She says I'm strong, that I'm her pride,
In every like and dislike, she's my guide.
She remembers every detail small,
Sees beauty in me, through it all.

She's there when I need her most,
No questions asked, no pride to boast.
In rejection's face, I find her near,
Her open heart, my refuge dear.

In tiredness, hurt, or broken days,
Her embrace guides me through the haze.
Her love, a constant, pure and true,
In every moment, her light renews.

Last Echoes of Radha

In the twilight of my days, I find myself alone,
The world grows dim, and the stars softly moan.
Amidst the shadows, where memories start to part,
I hold the keepsake that you gave me close to my heart.

Its touch is a whisper of the love we once knew,
A fragment of moments when our souls first grew.
Through the years of longing, and countless tears that fell,
Your presence remains in the silence, where our stories dwell.

Each curve and crevice of this cherished token,
Speaks of promises unspoken, of vows unbroken.
In my final hours, as the earth bids me goodbye,
Your essence wraps around me, like a gentle lullaby.

I see your eyes in every dusk and dawn's embrace,
Feel your breath in the soft wind, your warmth in a trace.
With the keepsake clutched tightly, our love, I renew,
For even before departure, my spirit dances with you.

So as I tread the path to realms where shadows blend,
Know that my love for you transcends, without end.
With this precious memento, forever shall I stay,
Embraced in the light of our eternal, undying day.

Shadows of Grief

Mourning in Metaphor

"In the shadows of grief, we find solace in the language of metaphor, where words fall short and emotions overflow, weaving a tapestry of mourning that transcends the boundaries of expression."

- *Shree Shambav*

The Strength Within

In the dark chapters of our days,
We find how strong we are, in countless ways.
Never forget the trials you overcame,
For your strength will guide you through brighter days.

My mind, with knowledge, says, "Move on, proceed,"
Yet my heart, rich in wisdom, whispers, "Stay and believe."
For at every crossroads, new lessons await,
In uncertainty's face, our courage finds its state.

Paths diverge, and we part ways,
Unsure if we'll meet again someday.
Yet, we pledge support, hearts intertwined,
Acknowledging fate, our destinies aligned.

Success and failure, beyond our control,
In life's fleeting moments, we find our soul.
In shadows, strength is unearthed,
Guiding us through, from despair to rebirth.

Each crossroads teaches, unfolds the unknown,
In every decision, our courage is shown.
Hope blooms even on the darkest night,
As we navigate life, seek the light.

Embracing our past, we step forward tall,
Facing the future, answering its call.
In the labyrinth of life, we shed our gloom,
Knowing our inner strength will always bloom.

The Burden of Karna, The Wisdom of Krishna

Beneath the ancient tree, Karna stood,
A heart heavy with pain misunderstood.
"Krishna," he said, with a sorrowed sigh,
"My life, a curse—tell me why.

From birth, rejection clung to me,
A shadow cast by fate's decree.
My mother turned, my kin disowned,
A name unspoken, a life bemoaned.

Denied by Drona, cursed by Parshuram's ire,
Stripped of knowledge, I dared to aspire.
An errant arrow, a cow laid low,
Curses again—life's unyielding blow.

At Draupadi's court, I bore disgrace,
Ridiculed before every face.
And Kunti, my mother, in final plea,
Sought my silence to save her three."

Karna's voice broke, tears unveiled,
A warrior's spirit, yet sorrow, prevailed.
Krishna listened, his gaze profound,
A solace within his words was found.

"My dear Karna," Krishna softly began,
"Our lives are but threads in destiny's plan.
I, too, bore burdens, a cradle of strife,
Born amidst chains, hunted through life.

My parents lost, my childhood torn,
To hardship's rhythm, I was sworn.
Later, I learned, I was bound by fate,
To duties heavy, companions late.

But Karna, the truth I learned is clear:
Birth's chains can never hold us here.
It's not the trials, but how we rise,
That carves our path beneath the skies.

Loyalty, noble, yet must discern—
Not blind allegiance, but truth to earn.
Stand for dharma, its beacon bright,
The only guide through life's dark night.

Bitterness, Karna, is a treacherous call,
It traps the soul, ensuring its fall.
Instead, embrace righteousness' flame,
And rise above dishonour and shame.

Life is an arena of endless fight,
But it is our choices that grant us light.
Though storms may rage, stay steadfast, true,
The world will see the strength in you."

Karna's tears fell, but not in despair,
Krishna's wisdom hung in the air.
Beneath the tree, his burden eased,
A warrior found a soul at peace.

The wind whispered through branches high,
A promise carved in the boundless sky.
Though trials loom and darkness bends,
It's truth and dharma that transcend.

Beyond All Time

In love, they live—they do not die,
No tide can steal, no years deny.
No storm can break the touch so true,
A love once known, forever new.
Don't you think it is beyond all time?

Those who love are never gone,
Their essence lingers, laced in dawn.
Love defies both fate and space,
A force untouched by time's embrace.
Don't you think it is beyond all time?

I have not left; I walk with you,
In whispered winds and morning dew.
When hearts surrender, walls will fade,
And time dissolves in the love we've made.
Don't you think it is beyond all space?

So do not grieve, love does not end,
It shifts, transforms but will not bend.
Listen deep, beyond the sky,

You'll hear my soul—I'm still close by.
Don't you think it is beyond goodbye?

I have dissolved in rain and sea,
In air and fire, you'll still find me.
Love alone moves all that lives,
I am not lost—I only give.
Don't you think it is beyond all time?

Whispers of a Soul Departed

Losing someone from our midst—a sorrow vast and deep,
A fragile thread of life is undone, a flame no more to keep.
Though time moves on and duties shift in quiet, grieving sway,
Their presence lingers like a breath that never drifts away.

Shared laughter woven through our days, soft echoes still remain,
Imprinted in the corners where love once left its stain.
Within the hush of mourning hearts, reflection finds its place—
Each bond we formed, each life we touched, a sacred, silent grace.

The soul that journeyed onward leaves a question in the night:
Why do some stars burn briefly, yet blaze with blinding light?
Their absence hums a quiet song, a yearning none can see,
A hollow ache that pulses through the heart's eternity.

We send them off with trembling hands, with prayers and salted tears,
Entrusting them to realms beyond the boundaries of years.
No longer bound by earthly weight nor touched by mortal pain,
They dance in light unending, like a soft, celestial rain.

In the stillness after parting, where grief and grace entwine,
They live as whispered memory, beyond the edge of time.
Though gone from touch, they still remain—in spirit ever near—
A voice within the silence, a presence we hold dear.

A Symphony of Soulful Suffering

In the crucible of knowing, where pain breaks free,
Shattered are the walls, revealing what's meant to be.
A symphony of suffering, echoing through the soul,
Each note is a piercing truth, making the broken whole.

Can you, in awe, embrace the bitter cup,
Where pain and joy entwine, and sorrows sup?
Accept the seasons, the heart's ebb and flow,
In grief's wintry silence, a resilient warmth may grow.

The self-chosen suffering, a bitter draught we sip,
The healer's potion, from life's sacred script.
Trust the unseen hands that guide our fate,
In the silent chamber, where the heart contemplates.

The cup, though aflame, holds tears divine,
A vessel molded in the Potter's sacred design.
Within the crucible, where shadows dance and play,
Lessons of empathy and resilience find their way.

In the intricate tapestry of sorrow's embrace,
Seeds of growth are sown, finding solace and grace.
Amidst the shadows, where the heart takes flight,
Deeper emotions unfurl, in the canvas of the night.

Gems of understanding, forged in suffering's fire,
A profound journey, where the soul aspires.
In the silent echoes of pain's tender art,
A masterpiece born from the depths of the heart.

Whirlwind of Passion

Embers of Desire

"In the whirlwind of passion, where reason surrenders to raw emotion, desire becomes the ember that ignites the soul, burning away pretense to reveal the unspoken truths of the heart."

- *Shree Shambav*

A Journey of Justice and Integrity

In the realm of honour, a delicate dance unfolds,
Where virtue meets integrity, and stories are told.
Yet when justice is but a distant dream,
Personal honour may not be what it seems.

A hollow facade, devoid of light,
When honour's path strays from what's right.
Veiled behind excuses, unethical deeds,
It tarnishes morality's noble seeds.

Innocent lives, sacrificed in its name,
For honour alone, it's not worth the blame.
For true honour lies in the sanctity of life,
In protecting the vulnerable from strife.

But when darkness descends and evil prevails,
Honour becomes a weapon, with tales
Of oppression and tyranny, it's fraught,
A mockery of justice, it's not what we sought.

In dire times, when honour loses its way,
It's a duty that calls, without delay.
To cast it off, like a burden, with might,
And uphold what's just, in the darkest night.

For in sacrifice, in duty's flame,
True honour emerges without shame.
Grounded in righteousness, it stands tall,
A beacon of hope, for one and all.

The Power of Letting Go

There is a weight we carry, silent and deep,
Burdens of memories we try to keep.
Regrets are like shadows, clinging to our soul,
Holding us captive, not letting us be whole.

But there's a power in the release,
In surrendering to life, finding inner peace.
For the chains that bind are forged in fear,
And letting go makes the path more clear.

Let go of the past, let it slip through your hands,
Like grains of sand upon distant lands.
The storms of sorrow, the winds of despair,
Can only linger if we let them tear.

In the act of release, we find our wings,
Freedom from the pain that memory brings.
Happiness flows like rivers set free,
From the dams, we built inside you and me.

The heart grows light as the grip is eased,
In letting go, the soul is pleased.
For holding too tight to what is gone,
Blinds us from the light of the coming dawn.

Embrace the unknown, release the control,
Allow your spirit to feel whole.
In the space of surrender, true peace will grow,
The power of letting go — it's all we need to know.

So breathe deep, release your sigh,
Let your spirit soar, let it fly high.
For in the letting go, life begins anew,
And happiness will find its way back to you.

Return to the Source

Empty your mind and let thoughts cease,
They rise and fall like shifting sand.
Your heart will find a quiet release—
The tranquil touch of unseen hands.

Just watch the rush that never stays,
The world runs wild in fleeting chase.
But stillness shows the inward ways,
And leads you back to silent grace.

Does not each being, when it's done,
Return to where it once began?
The source of peace, the waking sun,
The joy behind the mortal span.

To seek that peace, you must be true,
Fulfil your path and walk unbound.
Destiny calls, both old and new—
With constancy, the soul is found.

And knowing this unshaken ground,
Is what it means to see the light.
To stray from it, where none is found,
Is endless ache in endless night.

In oneness with the Shambav flame,
You rise beyond both loss and pride.
Impartial now, no need for fame—
No fear of death, with naught to hide.

Your path is clear, the current kind,
You flow where higher waters move.
With Shambav deep in heart and mind—
You are the truth you once must prove.

The Strength in Yielding

When first we breathe, we're soft and small,
Alive with warmth, with hearts so wide.
But when we die, we stiffen slow—
The rigid soul is locked inside.

The trees sway, the blades of grass,
They bend with the wind and lean with grace.
But those gone dry and firm with age
Will crumble in their rooted place.

What breaks is what resists the flow;
What holds too tight forgets to feel.
The strong may stand, but not for long—
It's those who bend who truly heal.

An army bound by stubborn pride
Will fall despite its might and name.
And trees that will not bow in storm
Will snap beneath the sky's acclaim.

So never doubt your gentle form,
Or think your softness is a flaw.
The fierce may rise, then fall away—
But open hearts become the law.

For life and death are intertwined;
Each one gives way, each takes a turn.
To live is not to harden fast—
But be the flame that bends to burn.

Nest of Wisdom

In the heart of the forest, where shadows dance,
An old monk wanders in a timeless trance.
His soul, a vessel for nature's sweet whispers,
Guided by the rhythm of the earth beneath his feet.

Amidst the trees, a nest—a masterpiece divine,
Woven by nature's hand, a sacred shrine.
High atop a towering tree, it lays,
A sanctuary for life's nocturnal plays.

Drawn to its beauty, the monk draws near,
Offering silver coins, eyes bright with cheer.
But the shepherd boy, with innocence profound,
Refuses the offer, his resolve unbound.

Undeterred, the monk persists, his spirit bold,
Doubling his offer, his heart untold.
Yet the boy remains steadfast, untouched by gain,
For within that nest, innocence does reign.

With quiet resolve, the boy speaks true,
Of fragile lives and hearts so pure and new.
"No silver can heal," he gently imparts,
"The sorrow of a mother's broken heart."

At that moment, the monk feels a shift,
A revelation, a precious gift.
Wisdom alone cannot light the way,
But empathy and compassion pave the day.

With humility as his cloak, the monk bows low,
To the shepherd boy, whose wisdom does grow.
Five silver coins, a tribute to the truth,
A lesson learned in the days of youth.

As he walks away, beneath the forest's serene canopy,
The monk carries with him a newfound empathy.
For true joy, he knows, can only be found,
When wisdom and compassion walk hand in hand, profound.

Resilient Reverie

Blooms Amidst Adversity

"Amidst the harshest storms, the soul finds its quiet strength, and like a resilient bloom breaking through cracked earth, it reminds us that beauty often rises from the depths of adversity."

- *Shree Shambav*

Sacrifice

In the cocoon's embrace, a story unfolds,
A tale of sacrifice by a silkworm told.
In the silken threads, its essence spun,
A journey began with the setting sun.

A creature small, in quiet repose,
Silken whispers, the cocoon bestows.
Threads of sacrifice, each strand a prayer,
Weaving dreams, suspended in the air.

The mulberry leaves, a humble fare,
Yet, within the worm, resilience is rare.
Silent martyr in the moon's soft glow,
A sacrifice woven, a life to bestow.

Metamorphosis, a cosmic ballet,
A silkworm's fate, in silk array.
In the loom of time, destiny's weaver,
A sacrifice profound, a silk achiever.

As fibres bind, a tapestry grand,
The silkworm's sacrifice, a silent stand.
Each silk strand, a whispering hymn,
In the loom of life, a sacrifice is slim.

The loom's dance, a rhythmic trance,
Threads entwining a delicate advance.
The silkworm's sacrifice, a silent plea,
In the silk's embrace, a legacy.

O silkworm, in your sacrifice find,
A metaphor for the human mind.
In life's cocoon, we too transform,
Sacrifices made in silence, warm.

In threads of hope, resilience spun,
A silken journey, just begun.
For in each sacrifice, a lesson learned,
In the tapestry of life, the silkworms earned.

A Tale of Love and Loss

In the grandeur of marble halls, Alexander reigned,
With Eleanor, his love, their lives intertwined.
Opulence and prestige, their empire vast,
But fate's cruel twist brought their world to aghast.

A tempest of crisis, financial and dire,
Swept through the city, burning like fire.
Their empire crumbled, wealth turned to dust,
And in the wreckage, they felt utterly lost.

Once revered as a titan, now left all alone,
Friends and allies vanished, like shadows, they'd flown.
Desperate, Alexander sought solace below,
Among old friends and allies, who'd long been laid low.

But many had moved on, their allegiance betrayed,
By the shifting tides of fortune, they'd been swayed.
In darkness, Alexander learned a profound truth,
True wealth lies in bonds, not in gold's aloof.

Power and prestige, mere illusions, he found,
In the face of adversity, they quickly unwound.
Amidst the ruins, Eleanor stood by his side,
A beacon of hope, in the chaos, she'd guide.

Together, they vowed, to rebuild anew,
Not just their empire, but their relationships, too.
For they knew in their hearts, though fortunes may wane,
True strength lies in love, amidst loss and pain.

As they faced the future, hand in hand they'd stride,
Bound by a love that would never subside.
And in the ashes of their former life, they'd see,
The beauty of resilience, the power of unity.

So remember, Alexander mused with a sigh,
In times of importance, friends may draw nigh.
But when interests diverge, they'll soon disappear,
Nothing lasts forever, this truth hold dear.

For when you're up there, among fortune's throngs,
Remember those who stood by you in the long,
Nights of despair, when all seemed lost,
Their love and support, at no matter the cost.

Embracing Change and Healing

In a town where secrets lie deep,
Beneath the open sky's sweep,
A river once flowed, pure and free,
Through forests where creatures roamed with glee.

But winds of change swept through the land,
Nature's balance shifted, out of hand,
Forests felled, dams rose grand,
Leaving lives and dreams in shifting sand.

Amid this tale of loss and gain,
A farmer toils amidst the rain,
His fields were once lush, now bleak terrain,
He clings to echoes of an old refrain.

Yet in his heart, a wisdom grows,
From a sage whose words disclose,
Truths amidst life's ebb and flow,
That change is life's relentless throes.

WHISPERS OF ETERNITY

Across the land, where shadows wane,
A journey shared, through joy and pain,
To seek redemption, break the chain,
Of a soul once bound in silent disdain.

Forgotten truths and dreams unfurled,
Awakened by the river's swirl,
Where hearts find solace and worlds unfurl,
Healing scars of the past's cruel whirl.

In every tale of loss and woe,
A seed of hope begins to grow,
Through bonds of love, we come to know,
That healing starts where rivers flow.

So let us heed nature's gentle grace,
Embrace the change, find our place,
In life's eternal, rhythmic chase,
Where past and future interlace.

Learn to Love Yourself

In the quiet chambers of your heart,
Where whispers of doubt and fear reside,
A gentle voice beckons, a tender start,
"Embrace the soul you often hide."

In the mirror's gaze, reflect with grace,
Not just the flaws that seem to define,
But the beauty of your unique embrace,
A tapestry woven with love, intertwined.

Each scar tells a story, a battle won,
A testament to strength, resilience unfurled,
Like the rising sun, a new day begun,
You're more than your struggles in this vast world.

Release the weight of expectations so high,
Those chains of comparison that bind and confine,
You are enough, let the truth amplify,
In your authenticity, your spirit will shine.

Dance with your shadows, don't shy away,
For they're part of the journey, the path to the light,
With every misstep, learn, grow, and sway,
For love is a process, a beautiful fight.

Stand tall in your truth, with arms open wide,
Nurture your heart with kindness and care,
In the garden of self-love, let joy abide,
Water your soul with the dreams that you dare.

So, learn to love yourself, for you are a gift,
A masterpiece crafted, a story to tell,
In the depths of your being, let your spirit lift,
For in loving yourself, you'll learn to love well.

Wings of Freedom

In the realm of boundless sky, a lively bird takes flight,
Born into this world, its spirit burning bright,
Seeking to ascend, to soar with all its might,
Inhaling the freshness of the air, in the morning's early light.

Yearning for freedom, unbound by earthly chains,
No shackles of bondage, no rules to constrain,
Seeking happiness in the simple, the mundane,
Content with sustenance, in nature's gentle reign.

No need for medicine, no desire for prolonged days,
Living each moment fully, in nature's loving gaze,
With no prejudice for caste, in life's intricate maze,
In harmony with all, in the sun's warming rays.

No distinctions are drawn between the rich and the poor,
Seeking liberation from grasping hands that lure,
Embracing nature's rhythms, its essence pure,
Living with no expectations, it's essential to endure.

Yet, humanity quests for happiness in realms unknown,
Chasing artificial comforts, in towers of stone,
Blinded to the treasures that nature has sown,
Unaware of the beauty, in simplicity alone.

Yearning to cast off burdens, to break from binding chains,
To emerge from the shadows, where truth remains,
When will we awaken to the song of nature's refrain,
And find solace in its beauty, in its gentle domain?

The Path Through the Fog

Does life unfold in sudden tides,
With unknown starts and swift goodbyes?
The mist may hide the road ahead,
Yet in its veil, the way is said.

Does fog not teach us step by step,
To move with care where shadows crept?
If still we wait, afraid to stray,
Pain may carve the longer way.

Does fog not whisper, calm and wise,
"One task, one breath, let moments rise"?
Set forth, embrace what time reveals,
For truth is felt, not always seen.

What lies ahead, we may not know,
Yet now's the place where life must flow.
Not distant fears nor fleeting past,
But this one breath is all that lasts.

Trust the ground beneath your stride,
Though veiled in mist, walk side by side.
Each step will shape, each pause will mend,
For through the fog, the soul ascends.

Celestial Conversations

Dialogues with the Divine

"In the quiet expanse of the soul, amidst the whispers of the wind and the silent dance of stars, we find ourselves engaged in celestial conversations, where the Divine speaks in the language of the heart, guiding us on the path of enlightenment and understanding."

- *Shree Shambav*

A Journey of Surrender

From humble soil to lofty peaks, I climbed,
In endless pursuit, through life's maze, I chimed.
Thinking all I grasped was solely mine,
Blinded to the truth, lost in the temporal shrine.

I clung to riches, claiming them my own,
In folly, believing I reigned on the throne.
Yet swift as shadows, all slipped from my grasp,
Leaving me stranded, in the void's cruel clasp.

My toils, my kin, my treasures vast and grand,
Like fleeting whispers, vanished from my hand.
Alone I stood, amid the shroud of night,
Questioning my journey, engulfed in plight.

For I presumed permanence in realms mundane,
Yet now I ponder, what truly shall remain?
In depths of sorrow, a revelation swirled,
O Divine, you alone are my world.

You are my mother, father, beacon bright,
My kin, my friend, in the darkest plight.
You are my wisdom, wealth, and warm embrace,
In you, O Divine, I find eternal grace.

Divine Symphony of Eternal Grace

In the abode of joy and benevolence,
Lies the eternal truth and boundless beauty,
Your glory weaves through the boundless sky,
Adorning the cosmos at your divine feet,
The enchanting beauty and happiness all around.

Clouds chase the moon's tender light,
Stars shimmer in their ecstatic dance,
Planets and the sun bask in your grace,
Drinking deep from the infinite streams,
Unleashing founts upon the earth,
The enchanting beauty and happiness all around.

Celestial music mingles with leafy whispers,
The aroma of blooms carried on the breeze,
Stories and melodies dance through the trees,
Celestial beings swayed by your lore,
Inspired by the divine symphony.
The enchanting beauty and happiness all around.

Life flows ceaselessly, night and day,
Blessed by your tireless grace in life and death,
Our hearts soften with love, mercy, and devotion,
Wiping away the heat of our distress,
Showering us with boundless sympathy,
The enchanting beauty and happiness all around.

In grand festivity, the world hails Thee,
In prosperity, adoration, and complete submission,
Mesmerised by the splendour of your creation,
Immersed in thoughts of your great divinity,
The enchanting beauty and happiness all around.

The Eternal Stillness

If you can empty your mind,
Like a river surrendering to the ocean,
You will find a stillness deeper than silence,
A tranquillity that hums with eternal devotion.

Amid the endless rush of worldly desires,
Pause, and watch them whirl, relentless streams.
Yet feel the pull of their quiet return,
To the Source, the cradle of all dreams.

Each being, like a leaf in autumn's fall,
Drifts back to the arms of its sacred start.
To return is not an ending but a call,
A peace that whispers deep within the heart.

To know this destiny is to perceive,
The rhythm of constancy, the eternal glow.
To feel the pulse of light, we must believe,
Enlightenment's path is the one to know.

Without this knowing, life becomes a shade,
A fleeting shadow, sorrowed and confined.
But union with the Source will never fade,
It frees the heart and liberates the mind.

When you touch the Divine, impartial you'll stay,
A noble surrender, untouched by fear.
Life's shifting tides no longer hold their sway,
For in that stillness, the truth is clear.

Life and loss, gain and grief, simply unfold,
As ripples across an infinite stream.
In oneness, the vast mysteries are told,
And consciousness awakens from its dream.

For in that knowing, you find what is true,
Not just peace, but the essence of design.
You are a reflection of the endless hue,
A spark of the eternal, wholly divine.

Return to the Source

Empty your mind, let silence grow,
Drift like waves where soft winds blow.
The heart that listens, calm and free,
Shall know the peace of eternity.

Watch the world in endless race,
Chasing shadows, losing grace.
Yet every soul, through time's embrace,
Returns once more to its sacred place.

Do you not see, through joy and pain,
All must find their way again?
The source of peace, the boundless stream,
Where truth dissolves the fleeting dream.

But peace is not so lightly won,
One must walk till fate is done.
And to fulfill what life demands,
One must rise with steadfast hands.

To hold this path, so vast, untamed,
Is to know what can't be named.
Without this light, the heart will stray,
And sorrow reigns in endless grey.

Yet those who walk in truth unbound,
Find stillness where no fear is found.
In unity with Shambav's glow,
They rise beyond what time may show.

No fear of death, no chains remain,
No clinging to the loss or gain.
For Shambav is the endless tide,
And in that flow, we all abide.

The Path to Shambav

One who seeks to grasp the known,
Learns something new with each new day.
But one who walks the Shambav's light,
Unlearns the self along the way.

The weight of thoughts begins to fall,
Less remains with every breath.
Until the mind dissolves to stillness,
And silence overcomes all death.

You come at last to non-action's door,
Where nothing stirs, yet all is done.
No striving hand, no urgent will—
Just being, and the All as one.

The world is not a prize to win,
Nor forged by force, nor bent by flame.
It yields itself in nature's time,
Unmoved by power, pride, or name.

To master life is not control,
But yielding to its sacred flow.
You guide it not by pressing on,
But by the art of letting go.

So let the currents shape your soul,
Release the need to fix or fight.
For Shambav walks where stillness dwells—
In soft surrender lies true might.

Who Am I?

A young child turned with wonder wide to ask an old man still,
"Who are you, O silent sage, whom time has failed to still?"
The old man laughed—a tender sound, like wind through drifting sky,
"How can I name what I have shed, or name the reason why?"

I am not mind, nor fleeting thought, nor memory's fragile flame,
Not ego's pride, nor intellect, nor any changing name.
I am not sound, nor taste, nor sight, nor scent the wind may kiss—
Beyond all sense, beyond all form, I am eternal bliss.

I am not breath, nor vital force, nor form of flesh and bone,
Not bound by layers sheathed in skin, nor by the self I've known.
No limb or organ claims my soul, no weight my being bears,
For I am light, untouched by time, beyond both needs and cares.

No lust, no hate resides in me, no hunger or desire,
No pride to bind, no envy's flame, no ever-thirsting fire.
Not wealth, nor loss, nor worldly roles can tell you who I be—
I dwell beyond both gain and lack, in pure serenity.

Not sin nor virtue mark my path, nor sorrow, joy, or chain,
No need for chants or temple steps to wash away a stain.
I need no rite, no sacred text to teach me what is true—
For I am That which always was, and ever will be too.

No birth have I, no death to fear, no caste, nor name, nor creed,
No boundaries hold what I become, nor hunger, want, or need.
I am the all, yet not a thing—no shape, no line, no hue—
I am the stillness in the breath, the One in all of you.

Wings of the Soul

Let me open my wings and rise up high,
Like a bird released to the endless sky.
I yearn to soar where silence sings,
Beneath the stars with silver wings.

Dispel the shadows within my chest,
Let me sing where the meadows rest.
Not draped in songs that aren't my own,
But clothed in colors I've softly grown.

My spirit twirls with the morning light,
Along the streams, both clear and bright.
I chase the sun, the moon, the stars—
Embracing heaven with no bars.

I long to feel the falling rain,
To echo birds in sweet refrain.
To trace the arch of a fading hue,
And dance beneath the midnight dew.

I'll wear the clouds like robes of grace,
As thunder's voice ignites my pace.
Like rivers carving earth with might,
Let me drift through love and light.

Let winter winds rise from my soul,
Unbound, untouched by earthly role.
In hues of joy, let me ascend—
A soul set free that knows no end.

Serenade of Seasons

Poetry in Nature's Rhythm

"In the serenade of seasons, nature conducts a symphony of life, each note echoing the eternal dance of birth, growth, decay, and rebirth. Through poetry in nature's rhythm, we find solace in the ever-changing melody of existence, reminding us of the profound interconnectedness of all things."

\- *Shree Shambav*

A Journey of Wisdom and Wonder

In the realm where sea and shore align,
A tale unfolds, both grand and divine.
Within the sands, a miracle unseen,
Awaiting the dawn, where life begins to glean.

Beneath the sun's warm and gentle caress,
In soft, sandy nests, new life does progress.
Each egg is a vessel, a promise, a dream,
Carrying wisdom from the ages unseen.

As days pass by and the sun's rays dance,
A transformation begins, a subtle chance.
Within the shell, life stirs and grows,
Nourished by nature, its wisdom flows.

Emerging into the world, one by one,
The young turtles greet the morning sun.
Guided by the whispers of the ocean's call,
They heed the beckoning, one and all.

But who guides their steps, their journey true?
Is it encoded memory, passed through and through?
Or perhaps the cosmos, with its guiding hand,
Directs their path across the golden sand.

Yet in the heart of this tale, there lies,
A mother's love, beneath the skies.
Though she may not teach them to swim or walk,
Her presence guides them, in the depths they stalk.

And so, they venture forth, with purpose clear,
Each step is guided by a knowing, sincere.
In the vast expanse of the ocean blue,
They find their destiny, both old and new.

As they slip beneath the waves' gentle sway,
A sense of wonder, in their hearts, holds sway.
For in their journey, we see our own,
Guided by forces, both seen and unknown.

So let us heed the lessons, the turtles teach,
As we journey on, toward what we seek.
For in the wisdom of nature's grand design,
Lies the beauty of life, both yours and mine.

A Symphony of Nature's Beauty

In the garden where dawn first dances,
Upon the canvas of the waking sky,
Golden hues weave their spellbound trances,
As morning's symphony draws nigh.

Whispers of a gentle breeze,
Through dew-kissed blades of green,
Nature wakes with quiet ease,
A world in peaceful sheen.

Birdsong fills the crisp, fresh air,
Melodies of joy unfurl,
Each note a promise, bright and rare,
Of hope and renewal's swirl.

Flowers bloom with fragrant grace,
Petals soft as morning's kiss,
Reaching for the sun's embrace,
In a ballet of beauty, pure bliss.
Here, where light bathes the earth anew,

WHISPERS OF ETERNITY

Promising a day reborn,
The world awakens, vibrant and true,
In the glow of dawn's soft morn.

Oh, morning fair, in your embrace,
Hope and possibility thrive,
In this moment's tender grace,
Our spirits soar, alive.

For here, amidst nature's art,
A masterpiece unfolds,
A tapestry of the heart,
In wonders yet untold.

Let us pause and hold this gift,
In awe and deep respect,
For here, where nature's spirits lift,
Is where true beauty intersects.

In every petal, every beam of light,
In every bird's joyful call,
The divine reveals its might,
In the garden's gentle thrall.

What more magic could one ask,
From this world, so pure and free,
Where love and beauty bask,
In nature's symphony.

So let us cherish this morning's glow,
Let gratitude in our hearts adorn,
For in this garden, we come to know,
The essence of life reborn.

The Oak Tree and the Whispering Wind

Beneath a sky of endless hue,
An ancient oak in silence grew.
Its roots sank deep, its branches wide,
A steadfast keeper of the countryside.

No need for glory, no call for praise,
It stood in grace through nights and days.
Its leaves would dance, but not in demand—
Just partners to the breeze's hand.

The travellers came, their burdens weighed,
Found solace here, beneath its shade.
The weary lay, the birds took flight,
Its arms a haven through dawn and night.

Yet what it gave was not by force,
No loud demand, no charted course.
Its presence spoke in whispers clear,
A language soft, for hearts to hear.

The wind would pass, a fleeting guest,
A gentle voice, a quiet caress.
It carried seeds from branch to ground,
A wisdom sown, a truth profound.

For in the oak's unmoving frame,
A lesson lived, without a name.
To stand with purpose, firm yet free,
Is to live as rooted as the tree.

And those who paused within its shade,
Felt a peace that could not fade.
They left not knowing what had begun,
A journey inward, slow and unsung.

The oak and wind, in silent accord,
Taught more than sermons, spoke no word.
For simplicity whispers, where chaos cries,
And stillness blooms beneath wide skies.

So may we live, as the oak has shown,
Rooted deep, yet freely grown.
A quiet strength, a life unblurred,
A soul that whispers, like the wind's soft word.

The Bee's Wisdom

A little bird perched on a flowered tree,
Curious, it called to a humble bee:
"Tell me, dear friend, your life seems unfair,
You toil so hard with patient care.

From dawn to dusk, you labour, strive,
To craft sweet nectar, keep dreams alive.
Yet others steal the fruit you create,
Doesn't this fill your heart with hate?"

The bee paused mid-flight, her wings aglow,
And spoke with a wisdom the bird didn't know:
True, my honey may be taken away,
By hands unkind or those led astray.

But let me tell you, my feathered friend,
This truth endures till the very end:
They can take my honey, but not my art,
The skill that beats within my heart.

For the joy lies not in what they consume,
But in the flowers where I dance and bloom.
Each sip of nectar, each moment I weave,
Gives life a purpose I can't grieve.

Let them steal, for they'll never see,
The boundless joy in being me.
The art of giving, the rhythm of skies,
Are treasures no thief can ever disguise.

The bird sat silent, her heart set alight,
By the bee's wisdom, pure and bright.
For in the bee's simple, steadfast way,
She learned to embrace her work each day.

And so, the bee buzzed on with grace,
Unmoved by theft, in life's embrace.
Her honey was fleeting, her art her own,
A timeless truth the world had shown.

The Enchanting Beauty and Happiness All Around

In the abode of joy and boundless grace,
Where truth and beauty eternally embrace,
Your glory adorns the vast, endless sky,
The universe kneels, its treasures laid nigh.
The enchanting beauty and happiness all around.

Clouds chase the moon in their fleeting delight,
Stars glimmer in ecstasy, bathing the night.
The planets and sun, in Your radiant embrace,
Drink from the streams of your infinite grace.
The enchanting beauty and happiness all around.

Celestial music whispers through the trees,
Blending with floral scents on a gentle breeze.
Stories and songs travel with the air,
Urging the trees to dance, life to declare.
The enchanting beauty and happiness all around.

WHISPERS OF ETERNITY

Life flows ceaselessly, night and day,
Through ever-new streams along its way.
Your blessings unfurl through birth and death,
Soothing our hearts with each loving breath.
The enchanting beauty and happiness all around.

In grand festivity, the earth bows low,
In reverence and love, its devotion flows.
Awestruck by the wonders You've spun,
Immersed in the marvels of all You've begun.
The enchanting beauty and happiness all around.

O Source of light, O Creator divine,
Through You, the stars and the heavens align.
Joy spills over, eternal, profound,
Forever adorned by the beauty around.
The enchanting beauty and happiness all around.

The Wisdom of the River

He who clings tight to thought alone,
Becomes like wood grown dry and worn.
When storms arise and winds grow strong,
His brittle mind is swiftly torn.
For reason bound without the heart
Will break when soul and sky depart.

And he who drifts in unseen seas,
With eyes shut tight to all that's near,
Is like a ship in fog and foam,
That sails through stars but steers by fear.
Without a guide, he veers and spins—
No harbour calls, no journey ends.

True wisdom flows, not sharp or still,
It listens deep, yet trusts the tide.
It dances not on reason's edge,
Nor drowns in dreamings undefined.
Like water clear through stone and sand,
It shapes the world with a gentle hand.

The river doesn't stop to judge
Each rock it meets along the way.
It bends, it hums, it curves with grace—
It does not fight, nor does it stay.
It knows the sea beyond the bend,
And flows with faith until the end.

Awareness walks with every wave,
And surrender sings in every turn.
Together, they are not opposed—
But flames that in one lantern burn.
To trust is not to walk unwise,
But see through stillness, deeper eyes.

So let your spirit flow like streams,
Not stiff with pride, nor lost in haze.
Let thought and trust entwine as one—
Both are rooted deep, yet set ablaze.
For those who blend the mind and soul
Will find the sea—and still be whole.

Life Coach and Philanthropist

Shree Shambav is the visionary founder of the Shree Shambav Ayur Rakshita Foundation (www.shambav-ayurrakshita.org). He founded this institution with a lofty goal: to recognise human identity across gender, ethnicity, and nationality. Through this organisation, he wants to assist all communities in realising their full potential and the intrinsic beauty of life.

Shree Shambav, a Life Coach, is dedicated to supporting people on their journeys of self-discovery and empowerment. He assists people in discovering who they are, determining what inspires and drives them, and overcoming limiting ideas. His approach clarifies what one wants in life, assisting people through goal-setting and a step-by-step process for achieving them. He empowers people to make deliberate and responsible decisions, allowing them to identify their blind spots and evolve as individuals via the use of numerous strategies and tools.

The foundation's bold, uncompromising, and compassionate ventures are always aimed at initiating the "Inner Transformation" process. They focus on spiritual growth, personal growth, and self-healing while emphasising that true progress lies in "Inclusive Growth and Co-existence." This philosophy drives all their initiatives, encouraging a holistic approach to development and well-being.

Under Shree Shambav's leadership, the foundation has launched several impactful movements:

Shree Shambav Green Movement: This mission is to create a healthy, green, and clean earth through responsible water conservation and greening initiatives. The movement strives to make the world a green paradise by encouraging sustainable living and environmental responsibility.

Shree Shambav Vidya Vedhika (Vizhuthugal): This project aims to help students and children by offering training, books, stationery, and uniforms. It aims to provide the next generation with the tools and resources they need to excel both academically and personally.

Shree Shambav and his foundation exemplify the spirit of compassion, transformation, and inclusive growth via their work, which has a profound impact on individuals and communities around the world. His work exemplifies the power of acknowledging and nourishing the human spirit, creating a world in which everyone can reach their full potential and appreciate the beauty of life.

TESTIMONIALS

Journey of Soul - Karma - "We die in our twenties and are buried at eighty." Remember that nothing can stop someone who refuses to be stopped. "Most people do not fail; they simply give up." Shree Shambav deserves full credit. It allowed me to sit and consider what I might miss out on in life. The author has delved into every aspect of our daily lives. How can a seemingly insignificant change in these seemingly insignificant details bring us such joy? The Soul of Journey teaches you the "art of living" as well as the "art of dying."

Twenty + One Series - The rich cultural heritage offered a host in twenty + one short stories with incredible imagination, morals and values prevalent at a given time, influencing how people respond to a crisis or any situation. The author has recreated images with universal values and morals. The plentiful of fascinating from faraway lands would leave the modern play and story writers a cringe. The book supports trust and immeasurable values, instilling hope for the new generations.

Death - "Shree Shambav's 'Death - Light of Life and the Shadow of Death' is an extraordinary masterpiece that delves deep into the profound questions surrounding our existence and mortality. The book's opening statement, 'Nothing ever truly dies; it simply ceases to exist in one form before resuming it in another,' sets the stage for a thought-provoking exploration of death's multifaceted nature. Shambav's remarkable ability to navigate the philosophical complexities of death and our universal fear of it is both enlightening and comforting. This book is a testament to the power of understanding and acceptance."

Whispers of Eternity - "Reading 'Whispers of Eternity' by Shree Shambav was a transformative experience that left me captivated from beginning to end. Each section of this exquisite collection delves into the myriad facets of existence, offering poignant reflections on life, death, and everything in between. Shree Shambav's verses are a testament to the beauty of language and the power of expression, inviting readers to embark on a journey of self-discovery and spiritual awakening. Whether celebrating life's simple joys or grappling with the complexities of human emotion, this book is a timeless companion that speaks to the heart and soul of every reader."

Life Changing Journey Series - "Life Changing Journey Series II Inspirational Quotes" is a remarkable collection that illuminates the path to self-discovery and personal growth. With its inspiring quotes and insightful reflections, this book serves as a beacon of light in a world often shrouded in darkness. Each quote offers wisdom, guidance, and encouragement, reminding readers of their inner strength and resilience. A must-read for anyone seeking inspiration and enlightenment.

Learn To Love Yourself – "A Heartfelt Guide to Authentic Self-Love." "Learn to Love Yourself" invites readers on a transformative journey to embrace their true essence in a world often focused on external validation. Through ten insightful chapters, it gently reveals principles of genuine self-love, guiding readers to deepen their connection with themselves. Beyond surface positivity, it encourages the cultivation of resilient self-acceptance, from embracing one's unique qualities to setting empowering boundaries. With inspiring stories and practical wisdom, this book is a trusted companion on the path to inner peace, fulfilment, and joy, helping readers build lives that reflect their authentic selves.

The Power of Letting Go – This book has been a gift to my spiritual journey. Shree Shambav's insights into attachment, personal growth cycles, and forgiveness are enlightening. The concept of seven-year cycles resonated with me, helping me understand the natural phases of life. I feel more empowered to let go of what no longer serves me and step into a life of freedom and fulfilment. A truly beautiful read!

A Journey of Lasting Peace – "A Journey of Lasting Peace" feels like a trusted friend guiding you through the maze of self-discovery. The 18 transformative principles are both practical and deeply resonant, addressing everything from gratitude practices to the art of letting go. Each chapter is infused with warmth and wisdom, making it easy to apply the concepts to my life. I particularly appreciated the emphasis on physical health's connection to mental well-being; it served as a wake-up call for me to prioritize my health. This book is an invaluable resource for anyone serious about personal growth!

Astrology Unveiled Series – "Profound, Logical, and Inspiring". What stands out in Astrology Unveiled is the author's dedication to making Vedic astrology logical and approachable. Each concept flows naturally into the next, backed by examples and exercises. The insights into karma and life cycles add a philosophical depth rarely seen in astrology books. Perfect for anyone seeking spiritual growth alongside astrological knowledge!

The Entitlement Trap - "Thought-Provoking and Challenging" The book challenges readers to confront their own sense of entitlement, and that's not easy—but it's essential. The Entitlement Trap doesn't offer a one-size-fits-all approach. Instead, it's a thoughtful, layered examination of how entitlement can limit our growth. The chapter on "Defining Your Own Hill" was particularly impactful, as it pushed me to reconsider which challenges are truly worth pursuing. A thought-provoking read for those willing to do the inner work to create a life they can be proud of.

Whispers of a Dying Soul – "A Soul-Stirring Reflection on Life's Unspoken Truths" **-** *Whispers of a Dying Soul: Unspoken Regrets and Unlived Dreams"* is a deeply moving exploration of the unexpressed emotions and unfulfilled aspirations that shape our lives in ways we often don't realise. This book invites readers to confront the powerful, often hidden impact of regret while guiding them through a journey of introspection and healing. Each page opens a space to reflect on the choices that define us—from moments of unspoken love to neglected passions—offering a gentle reminder to live authentically and courageously.

Whispers of the Soul: A Journey Through Haiku - is a mesmerising collection that speaks directly to the heart. Each haiku is a delicate brushstroke capturing life's fleeting beauty and timeless wisdom, inviting readers into moments of deep reflection and peace. This book is a balm for the soul, guiding us to find meaning in stillness and connection in simplicity. The themes of nature, love, and mindfulness echo universal truths, resonating with quiet, powerful grace. It's a book to be savoured slowly, cherished deeply, and returned to often. Truly a gift for anyone seeking calm and clarity in life's chaos.

Whispers of Silence - Unlocking Inner Power through Stillness by Shree Shambav is a rare gem that beckons readers to pause, reflect, and reconnect with their inner selves. In a world that never stops talking, this book offers a profound exploration of silence—not as a void but as a rich and transformative space.

From the first page, Shree Shambav's writing resonates deeply, blending scientific insights with spiritual wisdom in a way that feels both universal and deeply personal. The author's ability to bridge the tangible and the transcendent makes this book an invaluable guide for anyone navigating the chaos of modern life.

ACKNOWLEDGEMENTS

To my grandfathers, grandmothers, mothers, fathers, aunts, uncles, neighbours, sisters, brothers, friends, and teachers they poured in endless moral stories, retellings of Ramayana, Mahabharata, Puranas, Upanishads, and so on.

My teachers, neighbours, and kindred souls. Who provided us with a stage to perform wonderful Puranic stories and were gracious enough to acknowledge our efforts.

The artists and translators of epics have served as a source of inspiration, invigorating our spirits, making these works accessible, and enabling us to grasp the profound depths and deeper dimensions they contain.

I also cherish the stimulating conversations; I had with my wonderful mothers, Punitha Muniswamy and Uma Devi.

Our family's youngest member, Aadhya, who always overwhelmed me with questions, inspired this book.

I would likewise prefer to express gratitude to Mr Sivakumar, Mrs Roopa Sivakumar, Mr Akshaya

Rajesh, Ms Akshatha Rajesh, Ms Apeksha Prabhu, Mr Akanksh Prabhu, Mr Nikash Sarasambi, and Mrs Spoorthi Nikash for their valuable inputs.

I must thank Mr Rajesh, Mr Savan Prabhu, Mrs Revathi Rajesh, Mrs Rajani Sarasambi, and Mrs Manju Reshma, who encouraged me and often suggested writing a book. Their unwavering belief that I had something valuable to offer kept me going during my writing sessions.

Love you all,

Shree Shambav

www.shambav.org

shreeshambav@gmail.com

BOOKS BY – AUTHOR

Journey of Soul - KARMA

"Journey of Soul – Karma" is a heartfelt exploration of life's profound truths in our increasingly complex world. Addressing challenges, inequalities, and the quest for meaning, this book brings the timeless concept of Karma into focus. It emphasizes Karma not merely as philosophy, but as a guiding principle for our daily lives, inspiring us to walk a path of integrity and purpose. Through this journey, readers gain insights into how actions shape destinies, encouraging a life aligned with truth and compassion. It's a beacon for those seeking a deeper, more fulfilled existence.

Death - Light of Life and the Shadow of Death

In *Light of Life and the Shadow of Death*, the enigma of mortality is approached with clarity and compassion. Death is an inevitable certainty, yet it casts a lingering shadow of fear over our lives, stirring grief and despair as we strive to prolong our time on earth. This profound work examines the fate of departed souls and the heavy emotions we attach to loss. Yet, it offers a path toward accepting death and finding peace amid life's uncertainties. Exploring our origins, ethical values, and purpose it unveils the sustaining truth of existence. The shadow of death, though daunting, is reframed as a shared, universal experience—one that calls us to confront our deepest fears with wisdom and grace.

Whispers of Eternity 150 Plus - A Symphony of Soulful Verses

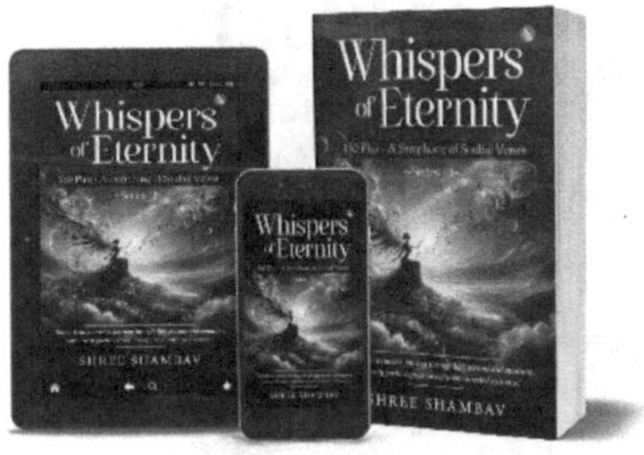

Step into the soul-stirring world of *Whispers of Eternity* by Shree Shambav, a collection of over 150 poems that capture the essence of the human experience. Divided into sections like "Through the Seasons," "Whispers of Hope," and "Threads of Unity," the book journeys through life's phases, emotions, and the universal connections that bind us all. Shree Shambav's verses touch upon nature, love, and spirituality, inspiring readers to find beauty in the everyday. Each poem is a finely crafted reflection, rich with insight and depth. *Whispers of Eternity* invites readers to pause, reflect, and embark on a timeless journey through the landscapes of the heart and soul.

Life Changing Journey Series I and II

In Life Changing Journey - 365 Inspirational Quotes Series I, Shree Shambav curates a powerful collection of 365 original quotes across fourteen chapters, each crafted to touch the heart of our daily lives. More than a simple compilation, this series speaks directly to personal experiences with wisdom and depth. Quotes like, "The most beautiful things are unseen but can be felt," echo the quiet beauty of life's intangible moments. Another, "Giving up is easier; holding oneself up is wiser," provides a guiding light in challenging times. Life Changing Journey reveals the transformative power of carefully chosen words, inspiring readers to find strength and new perspectives on their paths. Through Shree Shambav's work, readers are reminded of the wisdom and resilience hidden within each day.

Twenty + One - 21 Short Stories Series I and II

In *Twenty + One - Short Stories*, Shree Shambav brings to life the often-overlooked characters of nature—trees, animals, and mountains—revealing their intrinsic worth beyond mere utility. With poetic personification, he gives voice to these silent beings, some of whom are lucky enough to have names, titles, and rare human protection. Mountains, usually seen as mere landmarks, are depicted with reverence, emphasising their enduring presence. The stories build a bridge between humans and the natural world, showing that pain, grief, and resilience are shared across all forms of life. Shambav invites readers to empathise with the silent struggles of trees and animals, inspiring a fresh perspective on ecology and our responsibility towards the environment. This collection is a call to honour our connection to nature, encouraging readers to foster compassion and respect for all life.

Learn To Love Yourself

Learn to Love Yourself is a powerful invitation to turn inward in a world focused on external validation and superficial measures. Through ten transformative chapters, each offering a key rule for self-love, readers are guided to uncover their inner beauty, cultivate personal strength, and develop a solid foundation of self-acceptance. This journey goes beyond momentary happiness; it's about building an authentic relationship with yourself that fosters resilience, joy, and fulfilment. From embracing your unique qualities and practising compassion to setting boundaries and pursuing what makes you come alive, this book provides essential insights and practical guidance. Let *Learn to Love Yourself* be your trusted companion on this path, inspiring you to unlock the limitless potential within and find true inner peace.

The Power of Letting Go

The Power of Letting Go invites you to release attachments, fears, and expectations, guiding you toward true inner freedom and joy. With deep insights, practical exercises, and timeless wisdom, this book equips you to face life's challenges with resilience and grace. It explores the essence of attachment, embraces the power of seven-year growth cycles, and teaches the art of forgiveness as a key to a fulfilled life. Each chapter brings concepts to life through relatable analogies and real stories, making profound ideas both accessible and engaging. Let this book serve as your beacon for self-discovery and spiritual awakening, helping you navigate uncertainties and unlock your potential for a joyful, meaningful existence.

A Journey of Lasting Peace

A Journey of Lasting Peace is a transformative guide to self-love, inner peace, and personal strength, where Shree Shambav leads readers through 18 powerful principles for discovering their true selves. Each chapter explores vital themes, from the quest for inner peace and the importance of self-awareness to the healing practices of mindfulness and yoga. Through practical strategies, reflective exercises, and heartfelt stories, this book offers a clear roadmap to a more authentic and fulfilling life.

Whether you seek to embrace imperfection, establish healthy boundaries, or reconnect with nature, A Journey of Lasting Peace provides the wisdom to navigate life's challenges and find enduring tranquillity. Perfect for anyone on a journey of self-discovery, this inspiring work gently reminds us that lasting peace starts within.

Astrology Unveiled: Series I and V

Astrology Unveiled: Foundations of Ancient Wisdom invites you to unlock the mysteries of astrology, offering timeless knowledge rooted in the teachings of ancient sages. This comprehensive guide explores fundamental principles like Rashi, Graha, Bhava, and Divisional charts, making it an essential resource for beginners and intermediate students alike.

With logical explanations and practical applications, Shree Shambav skilfully blends ancient insights with modern understanding. Rich in examples, detailed explanations, and engaging exercises, this book serves as an illuminating path to mastering Vedic astrology.

Embark on a transformative cosmic journey, discovering how astrology can unveil your destiny, guide life's choices, and support your spiritual growth.

The Entitlement Trap: Get Over It, Get On It

Are you feeling stuck in a cycle of blame and dissatisfaction? The Entitlement Trap: Get Over It, Get On It offers a transformative path to reclaiming your personal power. This insightful guide helps you break free from the mindset of victimhood and empowers you to take control of your life. Inside, you'll discover how to redefine success, prioritize your true values, and live with purpose. Through practical strategies, you'll learn to embrace simplicity, connect with nature, and leave a lasting legacy. Get ready to shift from powerless to empowered and create a life you love!

Whispers of a Dying Soul: Unspoken Regrets and Unlived Dreams

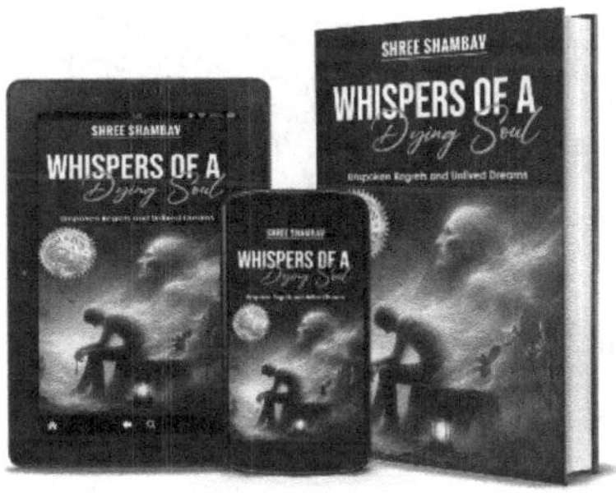

"Whispers of a Dying Soul", embarks on a profound journey that delves into the silent longings we often carry but seldom express. This powerful exploration uncovers the unspoken emotions that shape our lives—missed opportunities, unfulfilled dreams, and the quest for authenticity. Through heartfelt reflections and transformative insights, this book invites you to confront your regrets and turn them into powerful catalysts for growth and healing.

Whispers of the Soul: A Journey Through Haiku Series I to IV

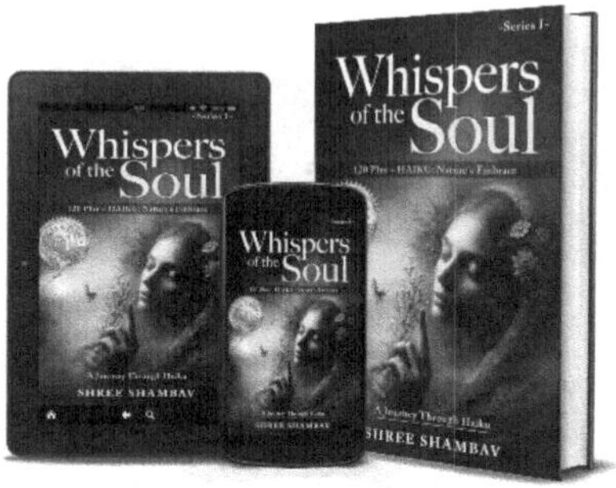

"Whispers of the Soul: A Journey Through Haiku" is a poetic invitation to pause and rediscover life's hidden beauty. This transformative collection of haikus explores themes of nature, mindfulness, love, and the human journey, offering profound reflections on universal experiences. Divided into five series, the book delves into nature's elegance, the depths of inner stillness, the tenderness of human connection, the passage of life's seasons, and the mysteries beyond the self. Each haiku captures fleeting moments with timeless grace, guiding readers toward peace, self-discovery, and a renewed appreciation for life's simplest wonders. This is more than poetry—it's a soulful journey.

The Power of Words: Transforming Speech, Transforming Lives

The Power of Words: Transforming Speech, Transforming Lives, illuminates the profound influence of our everyday language. This book explores how words can heal or harm, connect or divide, urging readers to embrace mindful communication. It delves into the "Sins of Speaking," such as gossip and judgment, while celebrating virtues like honesty, kindness, and authenticity. With practical strategies for transformation and a focus on the art of listening, Shree Shambav offers a roadmap to elevate our conversations. Perfect for both personal growth and professional development, this guide inspires readers to use their words to create peace, foster deeper connections, and lead a life of integrity and purpose.

The Art of Intentional Living: Minimalism for a Life of Purpose

In a world that celebrates more, The Art of Intentional Living invites you to embrace less. This powerful guide explores how minimalism can transform every aspect of your life—your space, your time, and your mind—by removing distractions and focusing on what truly matters.

Through simple yet profound principles, you'll learn to:

- Declutter your physical and digital space
- Prioritise what aligns with your values
- Create time for meaningful connections and experiences
- Cultivate a life of purpose, peace, and clarity

Awakening the Infinite: The Power of Consciousness in Transforming Life

In a fragmented world, Awakening the Infinite explores the power of consciousness to heal, transform, and unite. This book takes you on an experiential journey, revealing how awareness shapes reality and connects us to universal wisdom. Through spiritual teachings, introspection, and practical insights, it helps you uncover your soul's true purpose. Transformative practices guide you toward emotional healing, clarity, and personal growth. As you deepen your awareness, you'll forge a profound connection with yourself and the world around you. Embracing this journey leads to a life of mindfulness, authenticity, and purpose. Ultimately, it is an invitation to awaken the infinite potential within.

Beyond the Veil: A Journey Through Life After Death

Discover the Eternal Mystery of Life After Death What happens when we die? Is it the end, or a transition to something greater? In Beyond the Veil: A Journey Through Life After Death, explore humanity's greatest mystery through the lens of science, spirituality, and philosophy.

From near-death experiences to ancient spiritual teachings, this transformative book bridges the gap between the physical and the infinite, offering profound insights into the afterlife. Whether you're seeking comfort, answers, or inspiration, this journey will deepen your understanding of life, death, and what lies beyond.

Bonds Beyond Blood - Where love builds bridges, and bonds defy blood

Roots and Resilience is a poignant tale set against the quiet rhythm of suburban life, where a family grows strong through love, humility, and sacrifice. But when dreams collide with harsh realities and tragedy strikes, their foundation is shaken, and the true test of their bond begins. At the center stands a man, torn between honoring his past and forging a future amidst silent struggles within his marriage and the unspoken weight of grief. As the family navigates heartbreak, healing, and the quiet work of rebuilding, they discover that even broken roots can bloom again. This emotional journey is a testament to the resilience of the human spirit, the redemptive power of forgiveness, and the enduring strength found in choosing love—especially when life is at its most imperfect.

A Journey into Spiritual Maturity - 12 Golden Rules for Inner Transformation

In *A Journey into Spiritual Maturity: 12 Golden Rules for Inner Transformation*, Shree Shambav offers a soul-stirring path to self-discovery and inner peace. Blending timeless wisdom with practical tools, this book helps you release attachments, embrace change, and live with intention. Through inspiring stories and guided reflection, you'll learn to nurture self-love, deepen your relationships, and find freedom in authenticity.

Each golden rule is a beacon, illuminating the way toward a more meaningful, compassionate life. It is not just a guide—it's a companion for your soul's awakening. Let this journey lead you home to yourself.

9 789334 285543

Printed at Repro India Ltd.